THEOSOPHY AND LIFE'S DEEPER PROBLEMS

THEOSOPHY AND LIFE'S DEEPER PROBLEMS

Being the Four Convention Lectures Delivered in Bombay at the Fortieth Anniversary of the Theosophical Society, December, 1915

BY
ANNIE BESANT

GYAN

ISBN: 978-81-212-1888-7 (HB)
First Published, 1916
Published, 2018
Published by

GYAN

Gyan Publishing House
5, Ansari Road
Daryaganj, New Delhi-110002
Phone: 011-47034999, 9811692060
www.gyanbooks.com
E-mail: books@gyanbooks.com

Printed at: G. Print Process, Delhi.

FOREWORD

THE lectures really need no Foreword. They are frankly propagandist, being delivered in the City of Bombay, on the occasion of the return to that city for the first time since the Anniversary held in Framji Cowasji Hall, on December 7th, 1882, with 15 delegates present. The little seed there planted in India by our Founders has grown into a mighty tree. May it continue to spread ever more widely its branches, and may its leaves be for the healing of the Nations.

ANNIE BESANT

CONTENTS

THEOSOPHICAL CONVENTION LECTURES

GOD

Friends:

Amid the excitements of the present National Week, amid all the Conferences on matters of importance to the Nation, amid the discussions—industrial, commercial, political—which are agitating this great City, and will agitate it during the next week, we, of the Theosophical Society, have ventured to invite you here to consider not the passing concerns of the moment but the perpetual concerns of the life dealing with the eternal interests, the life wherein alone permanence can ever be found.

I have chosen for the subject of our Convention Lectures, those great problems of thought which ever challenge the attention of the highest mind of man. That question of questions of the nature, of our conception, of God; the nature of man, his relation to the Universe in which he finds himself—the evolution of an intelligent spiritual Being amid the transitory phenomena of passing worlds; then that profound question of conduct, what is Right and what is Wrong? is it possible to find a standard of ethics? is it possible to find a canon of conduct which will guide us in that tangled path of action which is one of the hardest problems of human life? Then, lastly, the meaning of Brotherhood, on what it is based, in what it consists, what duties it imposes upon us, what is to be our attitude to our brethren on every side. These questions, that on these four mornings we are to consider, are not questions of the passing time, but are the problems that confront humanity at all the stages of its evolution. Not only is that so, but in this alone can we find peace, amid the turmoil of the world; not in the constant struggles of outer life may peace be found, but in the heart of peace which abides in the ETERNAL, that can remain peaceful in the midst of storms, amid friends, amid enemies, amid neutrals; only in the Peace of the ETERNAL may the human Spirit find abiding rest. When that centre is found, when that knowledge of God which is eternal life has been realised by man, then, and then alone, can action be wisely taken, not swayed by passion, not moved by prejudices, having nothing to gain which the outer world can give and nothing to lose which that world can take away; asking for nothing, desiring nothing, save to be an instrument of the Will that works for Righteousness, seeing in the world around us the field of action where God is working, and where we can be co-workers with God. There, and there alone, can you work above the guṇas, using them for the Divine purposes, but not permitting yourself to fall under the glamour of their phenomena; making use of all: of the passions of man, of the aspirations of man, of the good and of the evil, turning them all to send man forward on the path which God has marked out for human progress. That is the high activity which finds its expression in Service, and that can only be where God has been realised, and where the Spirit of man, consciously one with the Spirit Eternal, sees everywhere one Will, one Wisdom, and one Activity, and men, in all their different workings, the instruments whereby the Divine Will is worked out in evolution.

Hence, our study in these four morning hours is not apart from the day's activity, but is really the source, the spring, of that activity; and so, loving all because in all the Self abides; seeing the inner Self, unblinded by outer appearances; thus may work the messengers of the great Hierarchy that guides our world. It is to a treading of the path that leads to Service, it is for that, that I invite your attention to these profound problems of the spiritual life of man.

Now, to-day, we are first to consider the nature, the existence, of that One Life in which we all subsist, and the views that man has taken thereof.

Let me say at the very outset, that there is a common view to-day among many thoughtful, among many good men, that it does not much matter what a man believes providing that his conduct is right. That is a half truth, not a whole truth, and it is the natural reaction from the Middle Age view in Europe that it did not matter what a man's conduct was provided that his beliefs were orthodox. Such a view has not only been found in mediæval Europe, but also has been found in India herself. You will find among Indians to-day, as still among some Christians, that the all-important matter is belief in certain dogmas, and that where those are held conduct is comparatively unimportant. We all know men in all faiths who are orthodox, as it is said, in belief, but whose lives are worldly lives, and sometimes not even of a very high worldly character. Now, a century or so ago that view was so common that men were persecuted, men were penalised, because of a difference of theological views. If men did not believe, at one stage, the dogmas of the Roman Catholic Church in Europe, then their fate was, at first, the stake, then later the prison, and still later, slander, social ostracism, and disabilities under the law of the land. In England, that is now largely swept aside, and we have the opposite exaggeration : "Let a man think as he will; but let him be a good citizen, a good man." But that leaves out the profound truth that "man is created by thought, and as a man thinks, so he is"; conduct is not independent of thought, for thought is the spring of conduct, and so it is written in the *Bhagavaḍ-Gīṭā*, that "a man is compacted, composed, of his beliefs," and as a man believes, so he is. You have to make, however, a distinction between beliefs conventionally accepted, and the real belief, which is the conviction of the heart, out of which action arises. And so, I urge on you to-day that right-thinking on the great truths of life is a most important part of the whole of your conduct. The better your thought, the better will be your life. The truer your thought, the more candid and transparent will be your actions. But *remember that it must be your own thought*, and not the thought of your neighbour, not the thought of authority, not the thought of a book, however ancient and however sacred, not the thought of a great man, however true for him; the thought that moulds conduct is the thought of the actor, and every man is responsible for his own thinking; the repetition of the thought of another is useless and even mischievous. Be not then afraid to think, even about God Himself. Do not think it is blasphemous to enquire; do not think it is blasphemous to doubt. Doubt is the stage which comes before a larger and truer thinking. You doubt your past thought, because you are opening up new vistas of thought and the past is lying behind you. The man who never doubts never really thinks; and there is a wholesome, a healthy scepticism which is the forerunner of a nobler and a truer faith. Think as far as you can. It is true that from the very Highest thought and speech fall back unable to go farther; but as far as you can think, as far as your intellect is able to grasp, to investigate, to argue, think your freest and your noblest, and you will grow by your errors as well as by your truths. Do not then fear to think; do not fear to be called unorthodox; try your best to think truly and accurately, and trust in Truth, who never betrays her servant. The determination to think your highest, the determination to think your best, may lead you into some desert for a time, but there are gardens on the other side of the desert. You may have to cross many a desert, many a torrent which seems to sweep you away; but I, who ventured all to seek for Truth, who left family, friends, religion, because their religion had become to me untrue, I bear you witness that such unbelief is the way to a higher, a greater, and a serener faith, and that those who are unwilling to lose the life of the past will not be able to advance into the life of the future.

Now, let us, with regard to our thoughts of God, realise that there are two lines towards knowledge. The first is the way of the intellect, which deals with metaphysics, which deals with philosophy, which gradually lifts a man out of superstition, out of narrowness, out of ignorance, and carries him as far as human intellect can go. Along those lines exercise your intellect, think your best, but remember, that it is written that not by intellect shall the Self be found, and the path of realisation is not the path of the intellect. It is the path of the conquered senses, of the conquered mind, when in the "quietude of the senses and the tranquillity of the mind, the man beholds the glory of the Self". That is realisation: that is the only knowledge: that is Eternal Life. By the intellect we reach the highest philosophy, and let none dare to despise philosophy, which rises up to peaks of knowledge, which are the glory of the human race. But, on the other hand, remember that it is the pure in heart who see God. It is the conquest of the lower nature which enables us to breathe the air in which the higher nature lives; and not by intellectual research, not even by devotion itself, but by sinking into the depths of your own being, by searching within, there where the Self abides; by casting aside everything that changes; by saying to the senses: "You are not I"; by saying to the mind: "You are not I"; by saying to the highest intelligence: "You are not I"; in the silence, where the mind has naught to say; in the silence, where the senses are not heard; in the depths of yourself, one with the Supreme Self; there, and there only, shall you realise that you yourself are one with the Self Universal. A hard path, a difficult path, the outcome of the practice of lives of self-abnegation and of service; but once you have realised God, you can never doubt again. An intellectual argument may be overthrown by keener logic, by larger grasp of facts; but the man who once has seen the Face of God, he never again can doubt that God is, that God is All. That is the Self-realisation of the Mystic. That is the triumph, not of the intellect but of the Spirit; then the Spirit which is Divine recognises its kinship with the Spirit Omnipresent, and when once, as I have said before, you have found God within yourself, then, and only then, will you find Him in every one, in everything, around you. That is the triumph of the Spirit. That is the Peace of the ETERNAL.

And now, let us turn to man's conceptions of God, and see how they have changed. And, in doing this, friends, let us seek for the kernel of truth which underlies even mistaken beliefs; for, man is so constituted that no error can hold him long in bondage save by the truth that that error conceals. Just as you may have the husk, the shell, and the kernel within it, so in every error that dominates mankind there is a kernel of truth that gives it its nutritive power. Only when you recognise the kernel of truth will you be able to convince a man of the husk of error.

Now, looking back to early times in our race, we find what is called Polytheism; and that you practically find everywhere. You find it very very strongly in the first half of the Hebrew *Old Testament,* as is called the Hebrew part of the Christian Bible. If you read that, what is the God that you find? Clearly, a God of limited power, a God of limited knowledge, what in the talk, the jargon, of the day is called a "tribal God". In the early story told by the Hebrews, the conception of God is very limited. You find Him "walking in the garden in the cool of the day," and calling out to the man he had created: "Adam, where art thou?" You find him a little later—when men have multiplied and begun to build a tower which in their ignorance they think will reach up to heaven—saying; "Go to, let us go down, and there confound their language, that they may not understand one another's speech." For "now nothing," he said, "will be restrained from them, which they have imagined to do". And so, we read, that "the Lord came down to see the city and the tower, which the children of men builded," and he confused the speech of the builders, so that they were scattered abroad and could not build their tower. And the Babel of Tongues is a phrase in English, because it was the Tower of Babel from which all the languages on earth originated! You find him again with his chosen people, the children of Abraham, leading them into the land he gives them; and then you come across the remarkable statement that "the Lord was with Judah," one of the tribes, and he drove out all "the inhabitants of the mountain, but could not drive out the inhabitants of the valley, because they had chariots of iron". You see at once that you are in the realm of a very limited kind of tribal God. Of course, I know that in the days when the Bible was regarded as verbally inspired, as God's Word, they said these statements were an accommodation to the ignorance of man; but that is only the desperate effort of the believer in verbal inspiration to infuse the knowledge of later days into the form of ancient fables. You and I recognise at once that where thoughtful Christians are concerned, these are to them old ideas, that you have here the local God, the tribal God, and that the God of the Hebrews of the early days does not claim to be the only God, but only the chief one, the chief for his own nation: "Who among the Gods is like unto Thee, O Jehovah!" That is the position of the Hebrews, and they have their own National God. To go away from him is treachery to the State. To disbelieve in him is punishable with death, because it is treason to the Nation, and such punishment was not so much regarded as a religious persecution as a State penalty. As a State and social sanction, the worship of Yahveh was maintained among the Hebrews; it was the State, the National, Religion. He conquered the Gods of the Philistines, He fought with the Gods of all the other people round about, each with their own God.

Then you come to a new aspect. The people of Israel are scattered; they are carried away captives into Babylon. They come into touch with the great Theologies of the East, and then a new view of God is taken by their writers. You may draw a line in the Hebrew Old Testament between the post-Babylon, and the pre-Babylon views of God. That is done now by every scholar. The pre-Babylon view is that of the Tribal God, one among many; the post-Babylon view is the sublime conception drawn from a great eastern faith, and then we find poetic and splendid phrases regarding God. He is the "High and Lofty One who inhabiteth Eternity, whose Name is Holy". There you have a spiritual thought. You are no longer within the region of the tribal Gods. You are out of the region of the local Deities; you have passed on into a great and spiritual world, where God inhabits Eternity, and where, in another splendid phrase, it is written: "God made man in the image of His own Eternity." There you have the later conception, there the God Universal; and with that, one remarkable fact that you must never forget, that in the later writing God is recognised not as what we call the Author of good only, but the Author of evil also. It is written in the Prophet Isaiah: "I am the Lord, and there is none else; I form the light and create darkness; I make peace, and create evil. I the Lord do all these things." It is written again: "Shall there be evil in a city, and the Lord hath not done it?" You must realise that where God is seen as "the One," when there is "none else," then He is the Author of all, and not only of the particular line of narrow morality that belongs to the evolving human kind. So also in the *Bhagavaḍ-Gīṭā* you find the phrase of Shrī Kṛṣhṇa: "I am the gambling of the cheat." I shall come back to that in order to point out to you its meaning, but at the moment I only ask you to remember that in what is now called the Christian Bible, not in the Hebrew part of it only, but in the Christian part as well, you find that same conception of one "Light that lighteth every man that cometh into the world," that shows itself in every form, that cannot be divorced from anything that exists. And so, in a very splendid psalm, again post-Babylon, you have the psalmist saying: "If I go up into Heaven, Thou art there; if I make my bed in Hell, behold, Thou art there also; if I take the wings of the morning and dwell in the uttermost parts of the sea, even there shall Thy Hand guide me, and Thy Right Hand lead me." Heaven or Hell, what are they? passing phenomena of human evolution. If God is found in Heaven, he is also found in Hell; only in Heaven he is the Bliss of Unity with the Law; in Hell He is the Pain of Law disregarded, and that, in order that by the suffering caused by the onward rush of the disregarded Law, He may teach the lesson of obedience to the Law, the lesson which the man refused to learn by precept, and must therefore, for his own future safety, learn by experience. Now that idea is eastern. When the Christians wrote the New Testament, they narrowed this profound idea of God.

They brought also, those post-Babylon Jews, they brought also the Babylonian conception of an Evil Spirit over against the Good, the great idea in Zoroastrianism of the opposition between Hormazd and Ahriman, that coloured all the Christian concepts. The Satan of Christianity, the Satan of the Christians, is the Ahriman of the Zoroastrians. And so also with the Eblis of the Musulmāns. He is the enemy of God. There you come down, as it were, to the planes of practice. Two forces quarrel for the mastery and we call them good and evil, recognising the duality of the flesh and the Spirit. We take that duality, and we put one over against the other. We forget that the flesh is necessary for the unfolding of the Spirit. We forget that matter is the necessary field in which the Seed of Divinity shall develop into the manifest God, and so we lose the Unity. We live in the realm of duality, and we make opposites, as they are in practical life, of those two sides of Deity, the Spirit that informs, the matter that makes action possible. Zarathushtra has, behind his duality, that "Boundless Space" which is really the description of the all-enveloping nature of God Universal; and when we deal with Hinḍūism, we find there the explanation of those rather fragmentary truths that come down to us along other lines. We have finally that terrible blunder of the Christian, who makes God, all love—as in truth He is—giving forth from Himself—for He is the only creator, One, "there is none else"—the Spirit Satan, who is the embodiment of hatred; and you find, finally, that in the great struggle, according to the common Christian belief—which intellectual Christians are outgrowing, you must not forgét—you find in the final result of the struggle, that it is not God, but Satan that is the conqueror, for "the bottomless pit" is full to overflowing, while Heaven is a city with walls around it, and with a comparatively limited number of inhabitants. But that is not the deeper teaching of Christianity; it is the crude popular view. If you go through the writings of S. Paul, what is written there? You find it is written that the day shall come when the Son, who is God, shall be "subject to Him who put all things under Him, and God shall be all in all"—God in Satan, God in Hell, God in the wicked, evolving them to righteousness. And so in the very centre of the Christian teaching you find that "God is all and in all," and is it not also written in *Al Qurān*, which largely reflects the popular necessary teachings of the time, is it not written by the great Prophet of Arabia, that "All shall perish, save His Face"? Everywhere is God; God is everything; in everything He is the ultimate good, the inevitable fate of man.

But now what does this Polytheism mean? There is a truth in it. For every Nation has its own Ḍeva, as we should say; its own Angel, as the Christian and Musalmān would say. These subordinate hosts, these Angels and Archangels, these Ḍevas and Ḍevīs, they are all superhuman intelligences, working out the will of God the Supreme. Think for a moment of Astronomy. There was a time when this little world was the centre of the Solar System, when fixed, with the Waters below and the Waters above, the Sun, the Moon, the Stars also, circled around our Globe. Science gradually found out that the universe was larger than the Solar System; that the Universe had many Suns and many systems. It found out that our globe went round the Sun and not the Sun round our globe. The world was lifted out of this position of superiority and thrown out into space, one among myriads of worlds; that was the heresy for which Giordano Bruno died. He proclaimed the multiplicity of worlds, and that the Sun was the centre of our system, but that there were other worlds and other Suns. In the old days that was a frightful horror, for he turned everything upside down. What can you do with Christian teachings if our globe is one among many? Christ died for this world. Did God die for a grain of dust in an endless Universe? The whole dignity of our world was lost. Then they said that Christ ascended up into Heaven, but Bruno said that there was no "up" and no "down". Our world with space below it; our world with space above it. Where then is Heaven? Where is Hell? Where is Heaven? Where is the Throne of God? Where the right hand of God where Christ is sitting? Where did He go to on that Ascension day? Where is He to be found in this unlimited space? And so they said: "Oh! burn him, get rid of him, send him to find the worlds of which he talks." So they burnt him and scattered his ashes, and joyed that he was dead. But Bruno lived still although the body was dead, and Science, Science triumphed, although its votaries were burnt, were racked, were imprisoned. They took Galileo and forced him to his knees to confess that he had been mistaken; "and yet it moves," were the whispered words of the Scientist, who did not dare to face the horrors of the Inquisition. And so Science triumphed, and now, what do you find? Not only that our Sun is, to us, a stationary body and the world goes round it; but that ours is only one of many systems, and that all those systems and their Suns go round another Sun, and that is not the last, and again that is not the last; for all those masses of systems, they also go round a still higher Sun, and so concentric circles of worlds, of systems, of Universes, without end that human eye can pierce, without end that human mind can grasp; and so we begin to realise that the local Gods of the past, they have their places, all circling round the One who is the centre of all life, "the One without a Second". All Universes rise and fall in Him. All Universes are born and die in His immensity. No thought may limit Him. No mind may grasp Him. He is the All, the One, the Omnipresent, and His Life lives in the Angels and Archangels, lives in the Devas of all the systems, and in all they are His Ministers, carrying out His Will.

And so there arose what is called Pantheism. God is All and in all. Now there is a great difference between the Pantheism of the West as embodied in Spinoza, and the Pantheism of the East, that you find in the Veḍas, that you find in the Zend-Avesta, that you find in the old dead Religions of Egypt, of Greece, of Rome. The Pantheism of the West is one Divine Existence with certain attributes, the Spinozean Pantheism. It is the Formless Boundless Existence. Not quite the Nirguṇa Brahman, the "Brahman without attributes". His Pantheism is as cold and uninspiring for conduct, as the Nirguṇa Brahman would be if that were the last word of Hinḍūism. Infinite, All-embracing, All-in-holding, out of Space and Time, that is the central thought of every great philosophy, Musalmān, Hinḍū, Zoroastrian, I might almost say Christian—though that is more doubtful, for it is more rigid, and narrowed by being confined more or less within the conceptions of the Bible. If you go to the great Musalmān Doctors of the ninth and tenth centuries A. D. you will find magnificent descriptions of the All-God. In That is said to exist not only what has been, not only what is, but that which shall be, and all eternally existent, all that is conceivable, all that is inconceivable, all is in Him. It is the same as the Aḍvaiṭa-Veḍānṭa

—if you take away from that the conception of the Saguṇa Brahman, and the devotional side of Shrī Shaṅkarāchārya in his sṭoṭras—the One without a Second, embracing all, conceiving all, all-existing, one Now, without past, present, and future, nothing to be excluded. But then comes the next step, the Saguṇa Brahman, the "Brahman with attributes," that is not a second, but the One in manifestation. He manifests a part of Himself. Said Shrī Kṛṣhṇa: "I established this Universe with a portion of myself, and I remain"; all-transcending, all-embracing, the manifested God, limiting Himself by manifestation. And so Manu speaks of Him as "a mountain of light," the generating Light; the One with attributes, but the attributes belong to the manifestation. They might vary perchance in another age, in another Universe. Then there go forth from Him the three great manifestations, Will, or Power; Wisdom, or Self-Realisation; Activity, or Creative Intelligence, and that threefold manifestation, of Power, of Self-Realisation, of Creative Intelligence, that is the root of every Trinity, as it is called, that you find in the ancient and in the modern worlds. Three forms of Manifestation inherent in one Existence, the creative Power, that brings a Universe into existence, called Brahmā among Hinḍūs; the sustaining all-preserving Power, that maintains a Universe, all-permeating, all-preserving, that is called Viṣhṇu; and He into whom all re-enters, the Destroyer, the Regenerator,

He into whom all returns that a higher form may reappear, that is Mahāḍeva, Shiva, the Supreme Bliss.

Naturally among a people unmetaphysical and unphilosophical, you get a division which in truth does not exist. They see three different Deities and quarrel over them, where there is only One, showing Himself in the three essential forms for a Universe which comes, which lives, which passes; and hence you have the Shaiva and the Vaiṣhṇava fighting the one against the other. I saw the other day in the caves of Elephanta, the Arḍha Shiva Arḍha Viṣhṇu, the Hari-Hara, which is said in the legends to be the combination of the twain in one. A fanatic was worshipping one and depreciating the other, it is said, and the image of Viṣhṇu changed, and became half Mahāḍeva and half Viṣhṇu, and the double image smiled upon the worshipper, to remind him that the division was in man and not in God.

So also there are hosts of Ḍevas, for the eastern Pantheism includes the innumerable forms in which God-in-all expresses Himself, and so we have Polytheism in a higher form. You need not be afraid of words, for that is the all-embracing truth. Polytheism asserts the existence of the Ḍevas and Ḍevīs, who carry out the Will of the Supreme. "Not for the sake of the Ḍeva is the Ḍeva dear, but for the sake of the Self is the Ḍeva dear." Only as the manifestation of the Self is the Ḍeva seen, as you, in your turn, are manifestations of the same Self. But the Ḍeva is a more highly evolved manifestation than you are. These innumerable ministers of the Supreme Will, they also are manifestations of the One; they mar not the Unity. And so in the Veḍas you chant to all of them; and so in the Zend-Avesta you invoke them all.

Now the Western will tell you that all these Ḍevas of yours are the personifications of the elements; that Agni is not a being, but is the Fire personified. You must turn that right upside down, if you want to make it true. Agni is not a personification of the element Fire; but Fire, the element, is the material expression of Agni, his body, his vehicle, by which he shows himself in the world. And that is your key. Ignorance personifies an Element. Knowledge sees a Being whose material expression is an Element. Ignorance sees the physical. Knowledge sees in everything physical a manifestation of the One Self, showing Himself in a limited form for the helping of His world. And so the higher Occultist may address Agni, the Ḍevarāja of Fire, and, below Agni, countless hosts of those who are called Fire Ḍevas, or Fire Elementals, all expressions of his nature, all using a special type of matter in the world. Hence you hear that when the world was built, the elements came forth, and each had the Life-principle within it. Fire came forth, but Agni, the Ḍevarāja, was the Life-principle within the fire-matter, and so with Varuṇa for water, and so with Kubera for earth. You have within every Element, nay, within everything that you call a law in nature, you have a Life-principle, a Ḍeva, or Angel, call him what you will, names matter not, provided that you realise that the Self which works in you as man, works in all these Beings in ascending ranks of hierarchical power; but they all are expressions of the one Divine Will, and the One works in all of them, and "the wise see the One, although they call Him by many names".

Now there you have the whole truth: God is everything and in All. God is manifested in countless forms, in countless grades of living intelligences, and each has its own place, and the Ḍevas come forth from Brahmā, as later from Him come forth vegetables and animals and men. There is only the One Life, but it is manifest in infinite forms—Pantheism-cum-Polytheism, God-in-a-Universe. Now, if you realise that, if you understand that, all these many Ḍevas and Ḍevīs, these many Angels and Archangels, are only expressions, phenomena, manifestations, of the One, just as you are. Then, you will realise that all these, carrying out the Divine Will, are the hearers of prayer, are the guardians of mankind; some are guardians of Nations, others the guardians of special areas smaller than Nations, but all are agents of the One. When the peasant prays to the form that he worships, and asks for help, that is really a prayer to the One Supreme, which is answered by His minister, the Ḍeva who is addressed by the peasant; and if you talk to the peasant here in India, you will find that most, if not all, of them realise the One behind the many, and know, that the One alone is God, although they appeal to those who are nearer in evolution to themselves, as they ask a Collector rather than the King. And so we begin to realise that Polytheism has its truth, and only needs to be understood. Then all Nature becomes living, beautiful, sympathetic, God smiles in everything. The thinker should realise it, and then none will ever blur the Unity by the multiplicity of manifestations. Thus you come to the whole truth, and find it living, exquisite, a perpetual joy. All Nature lives and loves. There is but One Life, but One Existence, but one Supreme Omnipresent Being. We cannot call him Spirit, because Spirit is the antithesis of Matter, and Spirit and Matter blend in Him. So we call Him the ONE WITHOUT A SECOND. In the boundless realms of space, in the infinity of Universes, that ONE is expressing Himself in countless ways, but all is a manifestation of Himself. He the One Thinker; from Him, all thought comes forth. He, the one Actor; from Him all activities proceed. All our human words of right and wrong, of good and evil, those are limited to the evolving lives in relation to each other. There is nothing that can be excluded from the One and Universal. In Him, all is well, all is highest and best. And, when we come to deal with Right and Wrong, we shall see how this works out, how it gives us a human standard, a standard by which we may guide our steps. But, for this morning, I will leave with you that Supreme Ideal : that there is but the One in All, in Everything; the lowest dust beneath your feet has the One within it; the highest Ḍeva in the highest heaven is but another expression of the One. You express Him, the animal expresses Him, the vegetable expresses Him, the mineral expresses Him. How else shall they live, save in Him who is life? How else shall they evolve, save in Him who is manifesting Himself through them? Be not afraid to love the world, which is one of His manifestations, one of His thoughts; but see Him everywhere and in everything, and so shall everything become spiritualised. Let Him speak to you through the world, as He speaks to you through the Spirit. He speaks in every breath of air; He speaks in every leaf on the forest tree; He speaks in the foam and crash of the Ocean's breaking billows; He speaks in the solitude and silence of the Mountain. There is none other. There is nothing else. He is the One Existence. And as you realise that, you share His power, and you share His peace.

MAN

FRIENDS:

I will ask you to remember the point at which we had arrived when the first lecture was concluded. We had studied the nature, the existence of God, and we had come to the point where we realised one all-pervading Life, the One without a Second, the One Life permeating every form from the lowest mineral to the highest Ḍeva, nay—the Lord of the Universe, Īshvara Himself. He also is an embodiment of the Supreme Self, showing forth infinite Power, Wisdom and Activity, the attributes of the Self, showing them forth in supreme measure. But even in Īshvara Himself, the Lord of the Universe, we recognise that He is an embodiment, and that, as is written in the *Bhāgavaṭa*, there are many Īshvaras, many Shivas, Viṣhṇus, Brahmās, each triplet the centre of a Universe, each the Īshvara of a Kosmos. Realising that, then, as our foundation, and that everything in a Universe, in its measure, is animated by the One Life, inspired by the One Energy, moved by the One Will, we then descend from those great heights to study one phase of the embodiments, that which we know as MAN. Realise that Man is only one grade in this mighty hierarchy of existences, that, beginning with the mineral, passing onwards through the vegetable, then ascending through the animal, culminates in Man, more and more of the Supreme Life shown out stage by stage. You may remember how the great commentator Sāyaṇa pointed out that the Supreme Self in the mineral shows out only the quality of existence. Passing onwards to vegetable and animal, He shows out there the attribute of consciousness. Passing onwards to Man, He reveals Himself in fuller measure—Man, who remembers what is past, who forecasts that which is yet to come. While man heads these ascending grades in our normal world, we yet pass onward in thought to the great hierarchies of Super-Men, of Ḍevas—Angels, call them what you will—then still onwards and onwards, ever in ascending grades of Power, of Wisdom and of Activity, until we reach those mighty Spirits who stand, as it were, around Īshvara Himself, His Viceroys in the mighty Empire of our system, all subordinates and ministers, who carry out the will of the Supreme Lord.

Now in this great Ladder of Life, Man occupies what we may call a middle place. The characteristic of Man is that in him there is a warfare of Spirit and of Matter, striving for the mastery. In the mineral, in the vegetable, in the animal, there you find

Matter is supreme; Spirit is most deeply veiled in the mineral, rather less veiled in the vegetable, still less in the animal. When we come to Man, in his lowest condition we find that Matter is still triumphant; then a struggle begins, and at last Spirit shows himself triumphant. Matter is spiritualised by the indwelling Life, and instead of being a fetter and a clog it becomes a vehicle, an expression of the indwelling, the directing, Spirit. The interest then of Man is that in all the stages of his long evolution the struggle is going on. First we see Matter is supreme. Gradually as Mind develops, the lowest manifestation of the Spirit, the struggle becomes marked; then slowly and gradually evolving, ever further and further, in the Saints, in the Sages of our race, we find the triumph of the human over the animal, the triumph of the Spirit over Matter; it is that mighty evolution that is the subject of our study this morning.

Where shall we begin? We must necessarily begin in the bosom of Īshvara Himself, whence come forth the human Spirits, the Jīvāṭmās. For is it not written that as millions of sparks go forth from the flaming fire, so do the Jīvāṭmās go forth from Īshvara Himself; or again, do we not find it said by Shrī Kṛṣhṇa, speaking as the Supreme Īshvaṛa: "A portion of Myself—Mamâmsha—a fragment of Myself, going forth into the world of Matter, draws round itself the senses, and mind as the sixth." There you have the definition of

Man. A portion of Īshvara Himself, a fragment of that illimitable Life, thrown down into the world of Matter, which incases the fragment within itself, which that fragment is destined to turn into a vehicle for the unfolded powers of God. As a seed is cast into the ground and within that seed lie hidden every power, every beauty, every possibility of the tree that sent it forth, so from the eternal Tree of Life of God Himself the seed is cast into the soil of our world, impotent, helpless, nescient—knowing nothing at first. But, inasmuch as it is a seed of God, it is destined to unfold Divine Powers, and to become in the course of ages the image of That from whom it has come forth. And so we find it written in the *Bṛhaṭ Āraṇyaka*, showing the contrast between the Supreme Āṭmā, the Paramāṭmā, and the Jivāṭmā, the human Spirit: "All-powerful the one, but powerless the other." In the one, all power manifests; in the other, every potentiality is present. And so, you find also in the later religion of Christianity, that it is declared by the mouth of the Christ Himself: "Be ye therefore perfect, as your Father which in Heaven is perfect." I ask all of you to realise what lies in those words of the Christ; as God in Heaven is perfect, such is the destiny of the children of men; not always to be weak and frivolous, not always to be childish and impotent, but to become, in the course of ages, *perfect* as God Himself is perfect. That, and nothing less than that, is the destiny of every one of you. You may delay it; you may retard it; you may wander in many bye-ways and lose ages of time; but what is time, however long, to you who are eternal, for whom there is no limit of space or time, inasmuch as your essence is the essence of God Himself. Nothing less than that, your Future.

But now, let us look at this Seed of Divinity and ask: How it is to develop, how it is to grow into splendour so illimitable? For though you be sons of a King, though your heritage be sure in the future, you may yet, if you will, grovel in the mire; you may, if you will, forget your birthright; you may think yourselves children of the dust, while you are children of Īshvara; but you must at last come to your inheritance, for the Divine Will in you cannot be ultimately frustrated, and your destiny, your Divine destiny, must be worked out.

Now, we have a fragment of Divinity embodied in flesh. Under what conditions, by what laws, is that fragment to evolve, to unfold its powers? There are two great laws under which that Seed of Divinity must develop into manifested God. The one, the Law of Re-incarnation; the turning of the wheel of births and deaths to which every one of us is bound; where freedom can only come to us by realising our Divinity; whence we may not escape until the law is utterly fulfilled. And the second, the Law of Karma, that law of the Divine Nature in which everything exists related, bound together, by simultaneous co-existence; hence, when out of that Eternity any portion of the Divine comes into space and into time, you have causation, where before there was simultaneity. You have what you call causation, which is only the coming into appearance and recognition of the real simultaneity of all. In God all is; in man all becomes; but that is the only difference; and what you call causation is nothing more than the unfolding in time, which is succession, of that which ever exists out of time in the Supreme. Let us then see how the law works, and it works through many stages, it works through endless ages. We have our Divine Seed—a child-Spirit, let us call him—born into our world. He is not left there alone, to find out by long experience only how evolution must proceed; for, out of previous Universes, out of past evolutions in other worlds, there come to the helping of these infant children of Man, Those who have passed through the earlier stages, and have become super-human in Their knowledge and Their power. There are two ways of finding out the existence of a law. One, the way in which, surrounded by the laws of nature that we may not change nor violate, unknowing that they exist, unconscious that they are around us, we are like a man in a darkened chamber, where there is no light to see his environment, who knocks himself up against one thing or another and bruises himself in the knocking. By the bruising, he finds out the obstacles; by the pain that he suffers, he finds that he can only move without pain in a certain direction. That is the scientific way. Every law of nature that has been so far discovered by Science has been discovered by experience which has turned ignorance into knowledge. Take Roger Bacon, one of the early chemists in the days when to investigate was heresy, in the days when to understand was crime. He was a monk, but a monk with the soul of a scientist in him. He experimented with chemical substances. He knew nothing about them. He did not know that putting these two together made a new and useful substance; that putting another two together made an explosive substance, that scattered everything around. He put together whatever he could find. What was the result? One time he was stretched senseless on the floor of his cell; another time a finger was blown off; another time an eye was blown out; onward and onward he went, with that dauntless courage, that interminable patience, which make the truly scientific man, who looks on knowledge as the supreme good. Struck senseless he came to again, and began again his work: missing a finger, he used the rest for new experimentation: when one eye had gone, the other remained with which he could still see. And, by such pain, by such loss, such infinity of dangers, Science slowly won its way to its knowledge of the laws around it. Inviolably, unchangeably, God manifests in Nature.

The result of the long experimenting is that now, when the young man goes into the laboratory, text-books are ready for him. A professor is there to warn him where the dangers of investigation lie. "Do not put," he will say to him, "nitrogen and chlorine together; if you put them together without certain precautions, you will find yourself in fragments and your laboratory will be destroyed." The boy in the laboratory now does not experience the dangers of earlier investigators. That, for him, is done. Men have come to show him the way, and the experience of the Past is the guide to the knowledge of the Present, and the warning to the dangers of the Future. So with Man. There were Professors, there were Teachers, round the infant races of our Globe. We call them Ṛṣhis; we call them Saints; we call them God-illuminated men; we call them Sages; Founders of Religions; and They said to infant humanity, as the Professor says to the boy in the laboratory: "Do that, don't do the other. Here lies safety; there lies danger. Take our experience as a guide, and you will realise the existence of the law; your happiness lies in your obedience, in your conformity with law." Hence, infant humanity started with the advantages of Sages to guide it who proclaimed the law.

Now, for a moment, put yourselves by imagination in the position of one of those infant races, hearing the words of the Teacher, and willing to learn. "If," said the Teacher, "you follow that course of conduct, misery will result." You may remember the words of the Lord Buḍḍha, that "as the wheels of a cart follow on the heels of the ox, so misery follows on the commission of evil. As the wheels of the cart follow the heels of the ox, so happiness follows on the commission of right." And why? because, as we shall see tomorrow, right is harmony with law, and wrong is discord with it. And, as the law cannot be broken, as the law itself is inviolable, the man who dashes himself against it is like the ship that dashes against a rock; the rock remains unmoving, but the ship is shattered into pieces. So is it with the law, the expression of the Divine Nature.

Now the recognition of law was helped by those declarations of the Teachers. For when a man, disobedient and careless, committed a wrong act, he suffered; and then he said: "I was told that I should suffer; after all, the Teacher was right; I have made myself miserable by disobeying the law." And the earlier lessons of man ran along these lines.

Let us see how it worked out. A savage. His passions are his guides. He knows none other. He wants and takes; he desires and grasps; but he is living among others who also want and take, who also desire and grasp, and, there is a conflict between the desires of one man and another. We will follow one man: He sees his neighbour's wife; desires her; he takes her; perhaps, kills the husband—he is quite a savage, remember. He sees in his neighbour's tent food that he wants; he strikes the man down, and takes away the food. And he thinks: I have done well; I am happy; I have gained a beautiful woman; I have gained food; I am no longer hungry. This is the path of happiness for me." But he has made enemies. The friends of those whom he may have struck down in his licentiousness, they are his enemies, and presently he has to die, perhaps is killed in revenge. But, what we call Death is only the striking away of the body in which the Spirit eternal is dwelling, and this ignorant creature, when the body is struck away, finds himself in the midst of people whom he robbed and murdered during his life on earth. He is surrounded by enemies; he finds on the other side antagonism and hatred; and he learns in the other world—the world we call Preṭaloka or Kāmaloka—he learns there that to do these things means sorrow, and that pain is the ultimate result of the desire unjustly satisfied. It makes a little impression upon him. But during his life, he has not only robbed and murdered: he has loved; perhaps he has loved the woman he stole; perhaps he has loved the child that was born of her. Those little seeds of love remain. The Spirit carries them with him as he passes out of the body, and when he has suffered in Preṭaloka the result of the evil he has done, he passes on to Piṭṛloka and to Svarga, to enjoy the good that he has accomplished; and the seed of love, selfish probably, desiring gratification, finds in Pitṛ-loka satisfaction, and the power to love increases. And where there has been a seed of unselfish love, perhaps where the wife was ill, and the husband sat up at night, tending and nursing her although she was no longer a source of pleasure, but only a source of trouble and annoyance; that unselfishness grows out of love, even the animal love, or lust of the possessor, that remains as a little bit of unselfish seed to bear flower in Svarga. When he reaches Svarga, and finds there again the wife and the child he loved, then that little seed of love begins to grow, and grows through the life, the heavenly life, of happiness that he leads, and that is transmuted into a greater power of loving, which he brings back with him to his next birth, so that he finds himself on a higher plane of emotion than that he lived on in the last.

Now in the savage the growth is very slow. Hundreds of lives sometimes pass and little change is seen. But where the Sages I spoke of are present, there the growth is more rapid, for there comes in the recognition of the law, and the understanding of the sequence of events. The man comes back again for many births, until he comes back as an average common-place semi-civilised man. As a savage, he has hardly any power of thought; through the lives that pass the power of thought has grown. And now, you come to a man who, in a comparatively civilised country, is born as an ordinary mediocre man—"the man in the street," we often call him. Now his experience is more varied. He has many loves and hates, many unjust desires, but also some higher aspirations; and as he goes through a life, the result of his own past, he gathers together fresh experiences, whereof presently more faculty will be manufactured. Just as a sea-gull, sweeping through the air, sweeps down into the ocean, catches a fish, comes up again and flies away to feed upon the fish, so does the human being, out of the great expanse of life in the higher world, sweep down into physical existence to gain the food of experience there. He carries it away through the gateway of death, and feeds upon it in the worlds on the other side of death. Again, more fully and more subtly than in the early stages of life, he reaps the result of the evil that he has done; but his mind is now larger, his mind is more intelligent, he traces the evil act bringing about the suffering, and that is imprinted on the tablet of the mind. Then he goes on into Svarga, and there turns over the good experience he has gained. The experience in love-emotion, that turns into higher powers of loving, greater desire to serve, greater recognition of the claims of others upon him, until he has formed a better and higher love-emotion, ready to return with him to his next experience of life. But he has also gathered much thought; he has gained experience in knowledge; he has exerted mental faculties. He gathers up all the mental experiences and these he works up into intellectual faculties. Is it not written that man is created by thought, and what a man thinks upon that he becomes? The life of Svarga is a life of changing experience into faculty. Every experience that you are making now, intellectual experience, you will weave into mental power on the other side of death. Whatever you may have gained, whatever knowledge you have acquired, that you carry with you through the gateway of death, and you work it up into mental power during your life in Svarga. You may have been weak in some faculty, in judgment, we will say, and you made many errors in judgment here: you suffer for them on the other side of death. You remember them in Svarga, and you build up that experience into an increased power of judgment, and you bring that back with you as an innate quality, and it shows itself in your childhood as part of your intellectual equipment. And, so with every faculty, with reason, with memory, with logic, with the power of understanding; not one of your efforts here is wasted; they all come back to you as food-experience in your heavenly life. You brood over them, you change them into faculty, and that faculty is yours for evermore. For that passes on into the intellectual side of the Spirit, as the emotions pass on into the moral, which is the wisdom side; and so, you come back to earth with higher intellectual power, with greater moral faculty. That continues, on and on, life after life, and when you are born into the world with high ability, it only means the many lives you have studied, the many lives you have laboured in, the many after-death periods during which you have assimilated.

See how the process resembles your life here, which is, indeed, its reflection on the physical plane. You take food; you are satisfied. That food passes down, and is digested. The nutritive part of that is assimilated, and your brain, your muscles, your nerves, all grow by the assimilated nourishment; and when it is assimilated you begin to feel hungry again. You have used up what you took, and you are hungry for more food, in order that you may grow again; and then, you have again another meal, and the whole process is repeated.

So in your spiritual life also. You take the food of experience; you digest it; you assimilate the nutritive part of it, and by that you unfold the hidden powers of the Spirit, and, when you have assimilated all, when nothing remains to be transmuted, then in the heavenly world you are hungry for more experience, and your hunger brings you back to birth in the world in which that hunger can be satisfied. That is the Law. That is the Law of Reincarnation.

As you grow more and more in stature, your growth becomes more rapid. And at last, a time comes, when you say: "I have had enough of this; I no longer care for power—it ends in disappointment; I no longer care for wealth—it is a burden rather than a joy; I no longer care for the things that break in the enjoyment; I no longer care for the things that perish in the using." And then there sets in the discontent with the transitory goods of this world; there sets in that which is called Vairāgya—dispassion. The objects no longer attract; and then the man that has this Divine discontent within him begins to seek for the permanent, begins to look for that which will satisfy; and there is nothing that can satisfy the Divine Spirit in man save God Himself, the Illimitable Life and Love. And so, as an English poet wrote—an old-fashioned poet:

> When God at first made man,
> Having a glass of blessings standing by,
> Let me, He said, pour on him all I can;
> Let the world's riches which extended lie
> Contract into a span. Then strength first made its way,
> Then beauty followed, wealth and power and pleasure.
> At last, when all was gone, God made a stay.
> Perceiving that at last of all his treasure
> Rest in the bottom lay.
> For if I should, said He,
> Bestow this jewel also on my creature,
> He would adore my gifts instead of me,
> And rest in Nature, not the God of Nature,
> So both should losers be. Then let him keep the rest,
> But keep them in repining restlessness.
> Let him be rich and weary, that at last,
> If goodness move him not, yet restlessness
> Shall toss him to my breast.

Now that is the truth. There is nothing in all this world that does not break in your hands, when you have it. God is like a mother, and He dangles in front of His children all the joys, the glittering baubles, that earth can give. And, in front of one He dangles wealth, saying: "Come, my child, and grasp the wealth." And the child, in trying to grasp, puts out his power, and his strength develops, and his will develops, and in the struggle to be rich many of the faculties of the man and the power of will are developed, and when that has been done, and the child grasps the bauble—it breaks. For the value was in the struggle and not in the possession, for the Divine Spirit in man. The Divine Spirit in man can never be satisfied with gold or wealth. If a mother took up her child and carried it always, as some foolish men would have God carry us, then when the child ought to be walking, strengthening its legs, tumbling down and picking itself up again, it would have been carried in its mother's arms, until when it was 6 or 7 or 8, it would be paralysed, and would never grow into a man at all. And so it is with God's child, Man. "Struggle," He says. "See all the beautiful things I have here for you." For God is in all the objects of sense. God is in everything that attracts; there is no attraction save in God, the only fair. And so, He hides Himself in gold, and He hides Himself in pleasure, and He hides Himself in Power; and He hides Himself in fame; aud when the child has exerted himself and gained the desirable object, God slips out of it and the attraction vanishes, and so we grow and learn. It is the only way. We grow strong, intellectually strong, morally strong, until nothing has power to attract save the one supreme attraction, God Himself.

And so it is written, that when a man becomes weary he begins to abstain from the objects of the senses. And then come the strange words: "The objects of the senses turn away from the abstemious dweller in the body." Why? because God is in them, and when they no longer attract they have done their work, and they turn away to educate some less developed man; and then, it is written, that the taste for them still remains, but even the taste for them vanishes away when once the Supreme is seen. There lies the truth. You feel distaste for the lower only when you have seen the higher. When you have seen the Supreme Beauty, the fragments of that Beauty down here can no longer mislead; you see God in them, and keep a grateful memory of all that they have taught you, in that they have led to the realisation of the God hidden in them, the treasure which remains. When you have gained the knowledge, the realisation of God, what has earth left, that earth can give? He is all power; He is all might; He is all beauty; He is all love; and you learn to know that nothing that has attracted you can perish in its permanent reality. Although the form may break, and change into another, it only increases your treasure in the riches of the Supreme. You love a woman; it is well; for love is the great purifier and the great uplifter of human hearts; but remember that her loveliness is but a fragment of the Divine Loveliness, and that all that attracts in her is the beauty of the Self shining forth through the beauty of the form.

> Not for the sake of the wife is the wife dear, but for the sake of the Self the wife is dear; not for the sake of the husband is the husband dear, but for the sake of the Self the husband is dear; not for the sake of the son is the son dear, but for the sake of the Self the son is dear.

But the wife and the husband and the son are rightly dear, because there is dwelling in them the glory of the Self, and that remains for ever, with all that has made it beautiful to you on earth; for God is Love, and love can never die; and all the loving and beloved Jīvāṭmās, that have been embodied in many forms, remain as your companions through the everlasting ages of the Future.

Now when a man has learnt Vairāgya, then comes the great period of Service. No longer does he work for anything for himself, but to carry out the Divine Will in Evolution. Has not Shrī Kṛṣhṇa said that He acts perpetually? Because, "if I do not act," He says, "all these worlds would perish." "I have nothing to gain," are His words. But they would perish, save for Him, and He goes on to say: "Let the wise man, acting with me, render all action attractive." Action is only a clog, is only a fetter, after man has gained all its fruit in experience, when it is not done for the sake of sacrifice. But when the action is consecrated to the Service of God and Man, that action becomes wings that uplift, and not fetters that clog, the advancing Spirit. And so, in the arrangement of castes that we have in India, there is one great lesson that comes out. The Shūḍra, the lowest caste, is the man who serves all. But the highest, above all castes, the Sannyāsī, what is he but the Servant of humanity, reproducing on a loftier plane the Service in which a Shūḍra is taking his first lesson down here? The Shūḍra learns service to others, and accumulates what he learns; the Vaishya learns to sacrifice material wealth in charity to others; the Kṣhaṭṭriya learns to renounce life itself in defence of others; the Brâhmaṇa learns to renounce all for knowledge, that he may teach others. Then caste has taught its lessons, and the highest of all services are the services done for the sake of sacrifice by the liberated Spirit, the Paramahamsa, the man who has gone beyond the illusion of the Separated Self. So wisely was planned the ancient order, full of true significance.

The only other point that you have to remember is that all this is done under inviolable Law. "As you sow, so shall you reap." There is a great verse in a

Christian Scripture too often forgotten by Christians: "Be not deceived; God is not mocked; whatsoever a man soweth, that shall he also reap." No use for substitution; no putting on of an imputed righteousness; no safety by a Saviour; you must reap your own harvest, you must work out, earn, your own salvation for yourself. But this remember: that your only limitation in taking up the strength of God lies in you, and not in Him. That is where the doctrine of so-called Divine Grace comes in. As the Sun shines all around you, as the Sun shines upon your house, you may close all the shutters, and say: "I don't want light; I shut my windows and my doors against the incoming rays of the Sun." So may you say to the Supreme Sun, the Light and the Life of the Universe: "I shut against you the doors of my heart; I don't want you to penetrate within me. I close my doors; I close my windows; your light shall not illuminate my Soul." And the answer of the Divine is: "Behold, I stand at the door and knock; if any man open, I will come in." There lies what men call Divine Grace. The grace is ever there, shining upon your closed shutters. You may shut your door; there is no change in the effulgence of the Sun. And so there is the Divine Light ever around you. You turn your backs upon it, and you say that it is dark; you have refused to see the Light, and you dwell in the shadow that you yourselves have made. Well, stay there, as long as you will. Play with the toys, as long as it pleases you. But know, that the day will come when the breaking of the toys will leave you desolate, and then you will open your hearts to the Supreme Love, and say: "Light, come in, and fill my heart with Thyself, for Thou and I are one, we were never separate; and I, the child of Man, recognise my birthright, and I claim, in the Self-realisation of my Divinity, the fruition of my life as Man."

RIGHT AND WRONG

FRIENDS:

The problem that we have to consider this morning is one of great complexity and of great difficulty. Confusion as to "What is Right," as to "What is Wrong," is unfortunately very general among all, even among educated people. The standard of Right, the canon of Right, that is a matter that ought to be placed on some definite principle, some intelligible axiom; and, if instead of such definite foundation, you do not realise on what the standard is based, the result is necessarily a confusion of conduct, a doubt as to how Right and Wrong are to be determined. And so, sometimes, almost in despair of a rationally intelligible law, you find people saying that Right is absolute, is always the same invariably for man at all stages of evolution. The result of that has been, both in the East and in the West, that a standard of conduct laid down for the Yogī, the Sannyāsī, is held to be the standard to be held up before the comparatively undeveloped man. The Sermon on the Mount, among Christians; the teaching of the *Bhagavaḍ-Giṭā*, of action without desire for fruit, among Hinḍūs; these are regarded as universally binding; and the result is a divorce between theory and practice, between the conduct which is actually followed and the theory which is intellectually accepted. You find a striking instance of that in the West, where the Sermon on the Mount, nominally regarded as binding on every one, is entirely put aside as regards the vast majority, and is held to have no bearing on National conduct, or the treatment of one Nation by another. You find, for instance, a Bishop of the Church of England who declared that if any Nation followed the teaching of the Sermon on the Mount it could not exist for a week. That is literally true. For if, when a man stole your coat, you gave him your cloak, the result would be that the thief would be doubly clothed, the honest man would go naked. If, when a man was struck on the one cheek, he turned to the striker the other cheek, then the oppressor and the tyrant would have free course, and the doctrine of non-resistance of evil would triumph over the resistance which means liberty and progress. And so, in the West, which has as a rule a fair amount of common-sense, and is not too much given to logic in practical matters, they resist evil, they resist the oppressor, they strike back when a blow is given, and they do not submissively bow to every tyrant and every injustice. Yet, unless you bring into accord theory and practice, you have no rule of conduct which in any way is an inspiration for life. Similarly in the East, where the doctrine is taught in the *Gīṭā* that action should be undertaken without desire for fruit. There you have a doctrine for the Yogī, like Arjuna, to whom the Song of the Lord was given; but if you say to the man of the world, if you say to the man who does not regard the Divine Will as the binding rule of conduct, "work without desire for fruit," you paralyse his activity, for there is no other motive sufficiently strong to move him to action. To work without desire for fruit means that your own will is so consciously in accord with the Will of God, that you work as earnestly for the benefit of the world as the ordinary man works for fame, for power, or for money. That is the highest rule of conduct; but if you teach the highest to the half-developed, you give them no ideal at all which is practical, by which they can guide their lives; and the result of that in India has been a paralysis of action, and a yielding unduly to oppression and injustice, as the Sannyāsī would yield. Now Hinḍūism, as taught by the Sages, was not of that type. Hinḍūism has always had a relative morality. The whole of that part of its teaching which divided society into castes according to evolution, the unfolding of the spiritual life, is a recognition that ḍharma, duty, depends on the stage of evolution reached by the man. The ḍharma of the Shūḍra is not the ḍharma of the Kṣhaṭṭriya or of the Brāhmaṇa. The Kṣhaṭṭriya is to keep order, he is to repress evil, he is to encourage good, he is to punish the wrong-doer; but the Brāhmaṇa, the ideal Brāhmaṇa, he ought to suffer any wrong done to him, for it is not his ḍharma to resist. And so, it is written, that a man by following his own ḍharma, he attaineth to perfection. That it is better to follow your own ḍharma though imperfect than to follow the ḍharma of another, for the ḍharma of another is full of danger. That has been forgotten in India, though, nominally, the caste system has persisted. And so, with the teaching of the Āshramas; the duty of the student, the Brahmachārī, is not the duty of the Gṛhasṭha, the householder, and when that is forgotten and when the duties of the householder are put on the shoulders of the student you have then a debilitated race of youth that is not allowed to grow to the stature of manhood which follows youthful celibacy. The duty of the householder is not the duty of the Vānaprasṭha; the duty of the Vānaprasṭha is not the duty of the Sannyāsī; for the Sages, the Ṛṣhis that built the foundation of Hinḍūism, they knew that morality was relative, and gave an evolving ethical teaching suited to the evolving children of Man. Let us then, with that preface, try to find some common principle to which we can refer Right and Wrong.

Realise, first of all, what morality means. I give it the definition that I have given elsewhere: "Morality is the Science of harmonious relations between intelligent beings." There is no morality for the mineral; there is no morality for the vegetable; there is no morality for the animal. Those are in the group under evolutionary law which compels them to go forward by the tremendous struggle for existence. By that struggle certain qualities are evolved—the qualities which are the bases of the humanity which is to be born into the world. There is a stage where there is no morality; where the creature is not immoral, but, is not-moral, is unmoral—without morality. He has not reached the stage where conscious obedience to law is possible for him; and so, as he is without the knowledge of good and evil, you cannot claim from him obedience to a law of Right and Wrong. Not only so, but taking that as our first point—that there is a stage where morality cannot exist because of the want of self-consciousness—the next point that you must realise, in establishing a Science of Morality, is a clear understanding of the meaning of the word "law". Now "law" may be a command made by a human legislature, or made arbitrarily by the ruler of a Nation, changeable, therefore, with an arbitrary penalty attached to its transgression. But the moral law, like all laws of Nature, is not a command either to do, or not to do. It is a declaration of conditions which produce certain definite results. Chemical law does not tell you, you *must* put hydrogen and oxygen together and produce water. You may produce water or not as you like; you are perfectly free to make it or not to make it; but the law is that if you put hydrogen and oxygen together at a certain temperature under a certain pressure, then you must produce water. It is a statement of conditions, followed by unchangeable result. A law of Nature, therefore, is not violable. You cannot change it. Nothing can prevent the formation of water, if only the conditions for its production are present. Nothing can ever produce water unless the conditions for its production are present. You cannot change it; that is a law. But, according to your knowledge of law is your freedom in a realm of law. The ignorant man goes about in Nature buffeted by her laws, crushed by some, helped by others; to him the happenings are matters of chance, for he knows not the laws amid which he lives. Cabined, crippled, rendered helpless, he stands before an inexorable Nature, and knows not how, or whither, he should move. But the man of knowledge, knowing the laws around him, walks with perfect freedom in a realm of law; he balances one law against another, he utilises laws that help, he neutralises laws that oppose him, and in proportion to his knowledge is his freedom; for, as it has well been said: "Nature is conquered by obedience." Obeying, he is free. Now the moral law is a natural law, not an artificial one. It is an expression, as are all the laws of Nature, of Īshvara, who is the life, the sustenance, of His Universe. The moral law cannot be broken; the moral law cannot be changed; it is the will of God in Evolution; and, by that alone may Right and Wrong be tested. That is Right which helps evolution forward; that is Wrong which opposes the Divine Will in Evolution. There is your standard, or canon, of Right and Wrong. Oh! you say, that is not a rough and ready definition, or standard. No; it requires knowledge. And so the Ṛṣhis, the great Teachers, have given certain commands—morals to be followed by the ignorant, based on the one supreme law of conformity to the Divine Will in Evolution. We are told by Vyāsa: "To do good to another is Right; to do evil to another is Wrong." We are told by the Christ: "Do unto others as ye would that they should do to you." But take those two moral commands, and see whether under all circumstances they should be obeyed. As a rough rule of conduct—yes; for the masses of people—yes; but can a King obey Christ's command, or a Judge "do unto others as" he "would that they should do unto" him? When he has a murderer before him in the dock, and he sits to administer the law of the land, may he say: "I must do to the murderer as I would that he should do to me, and I must not sentence him to punishment because I would not wish to be so sentenced"? All these general commands as to action are limited in their scope, are modified by surrounding conditions, depend on the position of the person. You and I have no right to lock up in a room another person because he has injured us; but the Judge has the duty of locking him up, if he has transgressed the law of the land and prison is the appointed punishment. Another precept was given by a very practical man, Confucius. He was asked: "How shall we behave? What word is there which defines our duty? shall we return good for evil, as the great Sage Lâo-tsze has declared?" And Confucius, being a practical statesman, answered: "Is not 'Reciprocity' such a word? If you return good for evil, with what will you recompense good? Recompense good with good, and evil with justice." Now there you have the law of the State. The law of forgiveness, the law of returning good for evil, is the law for the man aspiring to lead a spiritual life. It is a duty on the Path of Holiness; it is a duty of one aspiring to become a Saint or a Yogī. It is the law for the individual conduct which raises the man from the brute to the God; but for the State, that is not the law. For the Nation, the stage of evolution has not yet been reached which can return good for evil, and allow an enemy to overrun the country and to have his will upon the people.

And so, in dealing with morality, as in dealing with every Science, you must use your brains as well as your emotions, and you must judge the consequence of actions in order to guide your path.

Looking then at it in this way, we must see what "evolution" means. It means that at first progress is secured by inviolable laws of Nature, that press upon a whole class. As I said, the mineral, the vegetable, the animal, they cannot resist the law; they cannot evade it; they are compelled by an inner instinct to conform themselves to the law of their nature, imprinted upon them by the hand of Īshvara Himself, and so you have no mental struggle. The wild beast in the forest, he develops keenness, swiftness, shrewdness, cunning, because without them, he perishes. When you come to the savage, the law of evolution is very much the same. The savage is without the knowledge of good or of evil, and that is recognised everywhere. Most of you will know the Jewish legend, how God created a man and a woman and placed them in a garden, so that they might enjoy the fruit of every tree in the garden save the one tree that was forbidden, the tree of the knowledge of good and evil. Then comes in the curious point that God gives His creatures a command: "You shall not eat of that tree"; but, having no knowledge of good and evil, they could not know that disobedience was evil and that obedience was good; and, as the fruit was attractive and desirable, they ate and gained the knowledge, which they had been forbidden to acquire. And so you have the curious condition that the "fall of man" is brought about by his ignorance of Right and Wrong; he does the Wrong unconsciously, and so gains the knowledge of distinction between good and evil. Now while it would be a terrible injustice that their ignorance should be counted as a sin, for which any of us, their descendants, should perish everlastingly, yet if you look on the story as a symbolical representation of fact, it becomes most illuminative and helpful. For the first stage in the emergence of the human race from the innocence and the ignorance of the animal and the animal-man lies in the experience of good and of evil, which brings happiness in assonance with the law and unhappiness in discord with the law. The savage knows no Right or Wrong. You remember the most typical case of the Missionary, who wanted to point out to an Australian savage that he should not, when he was hungry, have eaten his wife. He was short of food, the poor man, and was very very hungry; his wife was the handiest form of food; he killed her and ate her. "Oh!" but said the Missionary: "That was very wrong," and as there was no word in the savage's language for "wrong," he said: "That was not good." "I assure you," said the innocent savage, "she was very good." There was no idea there of any "good" except physical gratification, and as the flesh of the wife stilled the hunger of the man, "she was very good," he answered. Now there was no Right or Wrong there. The man was unmoral; he only knew the gratification of his own desires; he followed them blindly; but that, as with Adam and Eve, was the road to progress. He would want his wife presently, and he would miss her. The gratification of hunger was a momentary pleasure, but the presence of the wife was a continual help and service. And so, presently, that man would think that it was a mistake to kill her: "I had better have been hungry for a few more hours, and have kept my wife." And the first idea dawns upon him that the gratification of a momentary want is not the path to a lasting happiness. Both are temporary, of course, but one is longer than the other. Now the first lessons of the savage come along that line. The white man gives the savage drink; the savage likes it; he gets drunk; but he finds in the morning that he has a very bad headache; if the attraction of the drink is greater than the fear of headache, he goes on drinking and drinking, until he dies perhaps in delirium tremens. And looking at it all, after death, the savages profit by that; and they say: "This drink makes us ill; this drink shortens our life; this drink brings unhappiness at last"; and they learn after very many such experiences that intoxication is Wrong; but they cannot learn this without the experience. They cannot gain knowledge without knowing the pair of opposites, one of which is good and the other evil; and all the first evolution of the savage depends on his gathering experience, which shows him that going with the law of health means happiness in the physical sense, going against it means unhappiness. Now the savage takes a very long time to learn this. But he is not left, as I pointed out to you yesterday, only to the gathering of experience. Some wise man, the Founder of a religion, or nowadays a Christian or Musalmān Missionary, says: "Don't touch drink; it will make you miserable." He breaks the command. How many Hinḍūs, how many Musalmāns to-day, forbidden by their religions to take strong drink, break the religious command and suffer thereby. How many Princes of Rājpuṭāna have died in middle age owing to excessive drinking; so that you find a number of young Princes succeeding to the gadi, their fathers having fallen victims to the curse of European drink. The old Princes in Rājpuṭāna, Musalmān and Hinḍū, are the men who have followed the law of their religion, and have abstained from strong drink. Is that not a lesson to the younger men who follow them? You can see the result of the lesson in the improved temperance of the younger generation of Indian Princes to-day. They have learnt the lesson by the experience of others, instead of by the bitter fruit of experience in themselves.

For the elders who have died, not only is there the command given by a religion, but there is the experience on the other side of death. Now of all the miseries which can follow a man into the world after death, of all the miseries, the results of drink are perhaps almost the most terrible. There is a constant craving, for not in the physical body but in the senses of the Sūkṣhma Sharīra, lie the craving, the desire, the longing for sensual gratification; and, if a man has been drunken, if he has been profligate in his life, he finds himself tortured on the other side of death by the drink he cannot enjoy, by the craving of the sex instinct which he cannot gratify. Torn by the agony of longing, frustrated by the impossibility of gratification, there is branded on that soul, as with a red-hot iron: "It is foolish to yield to gratification that brings about the misery that now I am suffering." He has to starve out the craving by non-satisfaction, and the agonies of starvation are his doom. And so is impressed on the lasting memory of the man the knowledge that suffering follows on the undue gratification of the passions of the body. That comes back in the next life—or after many lives—that comes back in an innate distaste for this form of sense-gratification. You say: "Would it not have been better that he should have been spared this long experience?" Nay, it would not have been better; for you are only finally rid of a craving, when you cease to desire that which gratifies it; and the teaching of pain kills the *desire*, whereas the enforced abstinence, not killing the desire, would ever leave you a prey to the possibility of temptation. That is why the striking of the transgressor by the disregarded law, is the veriest mercy in the long life of Man.

Most of you have been evolved without craving for drink; most of you, if you have touched it, have thrown it aside as distasteful. It has no power over you; it has no attraction for you; you turn away from it with disgust, as that which cannot tempt; and the only way of reaching that point is to have had experience of the evil, and to know that it is the womb of pain. Now out of this grows one great lesson for those of you who are more advanced. You know that sometimes, you who are fathers and mothers, you know that against all precept, against all training, against all prayer, your son goes wrong. You have told him: "My boy, to give way to passion is ruinous"; you have told him: "If you yield, you will suffer in your manhood." He disregards your prayer; he disregards your commands; the wild youth goes on; he will have his way. In that moment of parental agony, in that moment of despair, remember that doctrine of the Omnipresence of God that I spoke of in the first discourse: "If I go down into hell, behold, thou art there also," and realise that God—who loves your child more than you can love, more wisely as well as more intensely—has allowed that soul to go down into hell in order that He may meet him there in his degradation and his agony, and teach him by the lesson of pain, when he would not learn by the lesson of precept, that there is a law that none may disregard and live in happiness. For God is the Pain that comes to the transgressor from the disregarded law, as He is the Bliss that comes to the man who is in harmony with law.

Now if you realise these great truths, you will understand how morality must change with the upward evolution of the individual man. When you see wrong-doing in the undeveloped, when you see evil in the savage—whether the savage who is an anachronism in civilised society, or the savage who in his own native conditions—you will realise that that man is only beginning to learn the lessons of morality, and must learn them by dashing himself against the laws he knows not. And so, gradually, he grows out of the unmoral state into the beginning of the moral state, when he knows a little distinction between Right and Wrong, and often chooses the Wrong, because of the temporary pleasure that the yielding to the Wrong affords. And then he has the lesson I have just spoken of, until, within his innermost nature, he has branded the evil to be avoided. Now it is no merit to any one of us that we do not murder a man. We do not want to do so, because we have done it very often in the past, and have found that the fruit thereof was pain. We do not want to do it now, and the not wanting to do a particular wrong is the proof of moral growth. I know how often we are inclined to say: "Oh! How admirable is the man who struggles against evil." Yes. It is admirable for a man to struggle against temptation, to see him fighting against his lower nature. He is a hero in the struggle. But greater than the man who struggles is the man who has transcended the struggle, and who does the Right naturally, because he loves the Law and feels no inclination to turn towards wrong. That is not so often remembered. The man who has conquered in past lives, the man who has risen above the temptations that his younger brother struggles against, he is at a higher stage of evolution, for he chooses with full conviction the concord with the will of God. That means that the Divine Will in his own Spirit is emerging, and that quality, the Divine Will in the man, is the sign of approaching Liberation.

Come to another point, where you do not know in a particular case, what is Right and what is Wrong. To the more developed man, it is no longer a conflict between the "Right and Wrong" that he knows. It is a conflict between two duties, and he does not know whether of the twain is the one that he should follow. There you come to the agony of the opening Spirit, the unfolding God within, who is faced by two paths, and knows not which is the right one. Some arguments on one side, some arguments on the other. "Which of the two paths shall I take? How may

I know what is the will of God?" That is the agony of the Soul whose will is set to the Right, but who does not know the Right under the conditions which surround him. What does it mean? It means that he lacks experience. For Conscience, that which tells you "this is Right, that is Wrong," is only the accumulated experience of your past, which has registered certain facts in the nature that you bring into the world with you as that fruit of experience. You have murdered—you have suffered; you are born with the instinct that murder is wrong. You have robbed—you have suffered; you are born with the instinct that theft is wrong. That does not exist in the savage. Take a savage child, and you will find that your precepts carry him up to a certain point, and you can go no further. You can awaken in him the result of past experience, but you cannot give him a Conscience, an experience, which he has not yet acquired. But you, you have a great fund of Conscience, a compelling voice, which says: "kill not," "steal not," "don't give way to lust which injures another"; you take it for granted that is Right, and that knowledge is the outcome of your past experience. But now, you do not know what is Right and what is Wrong. Why? Because, you have not had the experience to enable you to judge in a new condition, to enable you to see the Right in an environment that you have not been in before. When a fresh step forward is to be taken, when a new knowledge is to be gained, what shall you do? You have to act. First, use your best intelligence; think as far as you can. Then try to put aside the bias which the inner desire is apt to imprint upon your thinking. Try to put aside all questions of personal gain, all questions of personal loss, everything which makes you more inclined to take one path or the other. It is a difficult thing to do, and it implies considerable training before you can thus neutralise the inner desires of your nature. Do your best; and then having used your intelligence, having put aside your desires, try, in that tranquillity of mind and senses, lifting up your heart to God, or Master, to see which is the higher path. Sometimes an inner voice will whisper to you and give you guidance; sometimes a Ḍeva may help you and suggest the better path; sometimes you are left to find your own way. Having done your best, decide; and when you have decided, act; for you have done all you can. Then watch the results; see what is the outcome of your decision; and you will discover by that outcome whether you judged rightly or wrongly. If you judged wrongly, do not regret. You did your best, and you have gained a new experience by the blunder, and it will help you in the future. If you have done right, you are stronger for the future; you have solved a new problem and gained a new knowledge. Sometimes you may come to a point in your evolution, where you have to face the question of following your conviction of the inner law of Right against every impulse that presses you to take a lower path. You have grown to the point where new ideals attract. You have begun to realise that the claim of humanity is greater than the claim of individuals with whom you are connected. You have come to the point to which all must come, to the point where to follow the Right is martyrdom, and where to follow the Wrong is easy and is regarded as praiseworthy by those around you. My Brother, if you have come to that point, be glad with exceeding joy; for it means that you have gone beyond the normal evolution of your race, and that which is Right to the men and women around you has become Wrong to you, who have caught a glimpse of a higher law. And then, surely comes the question: "Will you stand by the fruit of your glimpse, alone, unhelped, unsupported, unregarded? Will you follow Conscience that bids you take the path alone, or will you follow the voice of the multitude, still at a lower range of evolution?" It is the choice of the Hero; it is the choice of the Martyr. Better to die, you will feel, than to bow to a lower law than that which your Spirit has learnt to recognise. To tell a lie is to be debased; to tell a lie is to lose the vision of Truth; to tell a lie is to put a bandage round your eyes, and to refuse to see that which is already glimpsed. And if for you it is easier to face calumny, ostracism, the cold shoulder of friends, the hatred of Governments, and, if against all these things, you say: "It is easier to suffer than to lie," then you are taking your place amidst earth's Heroes, and you are serving your day and generation. But make no mistake; the choice is not as easy as it seems. The worst enemy of the martyr and the hero is the inner enemy, not the outer—the love that pleads with you to falter in your duty; worse than all, the inner doubt. "Can I really be Right, when every one around me tells me I am Wrong? Can I alone see what ought to be done? All these good men and women, honourable, faithful, good citizens of the world, tell me that I am mistaken and headlong. Is it not conceit, is it not vanity, to set my solitary choice against the wisdom of the aged, against the experience of my time?" Ah! that is a worse enemy than any outside pressure, for the outer you can resist, but the inner saps the very essence of your strength; the time comes when you are able to say: "Right or Wrong, whether it leads me to heaven or to hell, I follow the Inner Voice, which is the best guide I have; and, if it leads me wrong to-day, I shall know the Right by my blunder to-morrow." I know that means courage beyond the normal, but that is the courage that the Martyrs have shown, and posterity rewards them, if contemporaries destroy them. For it is true, as Giordano Bruno said, going to the stake: "To know how to die in one century is to live for all centuries to come." And so, again, he taught what he called "the heroic life". "It is better to try nobly and to fail, than ignobly not to try at all." That is the great inspiration for those who have caught a glimpse of the higher. Follow your own higher, whatever it may be, and whithersoever it may lead you; for the inspiration comes from the highest yet manifest within you, and not to follow it is to be a traitor to the Truth you see. Thus, by study of the Divine Will in Evolution, by trying to see where one stands in the long climbing upwards, every man ultimately, must be the supreme and final judge of Right and Wrong for himself.

But remember: you should not blame your neighbour because he does not see with your eyes. You should not despise those who think you are wrong, but weigh their blame, and see how much of reason there is therein. Remember also that in this struggle upwards, full weight should be given to the experience of the race as well as to your own. You should not despise nor flout those laws which keep the mass of the people in the path of decency and of good citizenship, and you should remember the warning of Shrī Kṛṣhṇa, so pre-eminently wise: "The standard that the wise man sets, by that the people go." To take your own road alone means a tremendous responsibility, as well as an act of heroism, for others may follow, unknowing, where you have deliberately chosen your path. Others less prepared by self-discipline and training may rush in after you where you have opened the gateway; and so, in your action, by which the blind must judge you, you must consider your circumstances as well as your vision of the Best. Only when to yield is treason to the Highest in you, should you set yourself alone against the world. "Tangled," said Shrī Kṛṣhṇa, "Tangled is the path of action," and that is true. Therefore you must develop your intellect; therefore you must train your will; therefore you must try to illuminate your judgment; no headlong, thoughtless action must be taken on the first impulse towards an unaccustomed path.

There is one thing that I have often said, and that I will here repeat, especially for my younger friends, whom I welcome to our meetings here. I would say to them: If you want advice, and ask: "Shall I disobey the customary law, and go my own way?"—then wait. The wanting of advice is the sign that the Spirit in you has not yet spoken with the compelling voice that you ought to obey. I have had boys come to me and say: "Shall I disobey my father? this refusal to obey seems to be the right path." My answer invariably has been: "My boy, if you are doubtful, as you must be since you ask me, then obey your father and mother, and see what the result is; for, when the Spirit speaks, no outside advice is wanted."

The great decisions of the Spirit are made in solitude, and they are not made by the advice of man. If you want others to support you, if you want the opinion of others to buttress you up, then the chances are, when the moment of stress comes upon you, you will quiver, you will say to your adviser: "Oh! you have advised me to do this; see what trouble it has brought, and I must suffer for it." And so, I have never advised, nor will advise, a great act of sacrifice. O crowd of thoughtful men and women, I say to you: "Choose your highest and follow it unflinchingly." But if any one of you comes to me and says: "Shall I sacrifice this? shall I sacrifice that? shall I disregard the other?" I say: "My friends, the decision is with you and not with me. Your own conscience must guide you. Your own intelligence must direct you. As I cannot suffer for you, I will not advise." For one has no right to impose upon another a sacrifice one is willing to face for one's self. I know my own strength and weakness. I am accustomed by many lives of aspiration to judge what path I shall follow. But shall I follow the path that I see to be Right for me, the path of suffering, and invite others to enter on it, who may not be prepared to face the pain? No; the decision towards pain must be made by the open vision of the one who affronts the suffering; otherwise, in the stress of the agony he may wish he had chosen the easier and the smoother path. The pioneer must know his strength; the pioneer must be ready for the stones that pierce his feet, for the thorns that tear his flesh. Let no weakling enter on the path of that higher, more strenuous, endeavour. We want pioneers. But we want pioneers of courage, of heart, of strength, of endurance, that no danger can daunt, that no peril can paralyse. Only such are worthy to come into the ranks of the pioneers, who make the path along which humanity shall march in days to come. And if you say to me: "Why should we go? Why should we suffer that others may tread smooth? Why should our flesh be torn that others may walk in ease?"—my answer is: "Unless the Spirit is so unfolded in you that the path of progress is to you the path of happiness, so that when the feet are bleeding, when the flesh is tortured, you can look up with a smile and say: 'Lord, I have come to do Thy will'; until the path to you is the only path of happiness, you had better tread the accustomed ways of the men and women around you."

For there is a time in evolution, when all wish for aught the world can give has vanished from the human Spirit; when there is no desire for aught save that God's will may be done on earth, as it is done in the higher realms of wisdom; when to be allowed to suffer in order that that Will may be done is a joy beyond all earthly joy, is a delight beyond anything that the world can give. Realise that the Martyr and the Hero die, because death is the most joyous thing that they can meet, knowing that by their death the world's progress is improved. Unless you feel this in you, then travel along the road that for you is Right; for the consent of the intelligence, the consent of the conscience, the realisation of God, these alone are the strength of the Hero; these, in the midst of the very flames of martyrdom, enable him to smile with joy, for vision of the future that he sees.

BROTHERHOOD

FRIENDS:

We have arrived now at the last of the four Convention Lectures, and I will ask you to recall for a moment the path that we have trodden on these three days.

First you remember we considered the nature, the existence of God, His all-pervading Presence, His all-embracing Love and Power. Then we turned to the study of Man, and we saw that man evolved, grew from a Seed of Divinity into the tree in the likeness of the father-tree, whence the seed was thrown into the world. That he evolved under two great Laws: the "Law of Reincarnation" and the "Law of Causation, or Karma". Yesterday, we considered the complex problem of Right and Wrong, tried to understand the tangled path of action, and to understand also how, by realising our highest capacities of the moment, we could rise higher and higher in Knowledge, in Power, and in Love. To-day we close our study by looking at the "Law of Brotherhood," trying to understand what it means, seeing what it implies, endeavouring then, in the understanding, to see the principles on which a stable Society may be builded, and to glance forward into the near future of Humanity, with the changed ideals which will illuminate the Coming Race.

Now, this word, "Brotherhood," has been used for many ages and held to cover many different ideals. First of all, let us take the fact that "Brotherhood" does not and cannot connote equality, save in blood, in essence; rather does it connote inequality of age and development. As you know, you have the proclamation talked of so much in the French Revolution, "Liberty, Equality, Fraternity," and it has been taken for granted by many that Liberty and Fraternity imply the middle term, Equality. Now what is meant by the word "Equality"? If it be meant that all men are equal in their origin, that every man is born of the Divine Nature, that every man ultimately will reach the manifested Divinity, in that sense Equality is true. We all come forth from God, we all return to God, bearing with us the harvest of our long evolution, having unfolded potentiality into power. In the beginning and the ending, men are equal, equally divine in their beginning, equally divine in their ending; there all men stand on a common platform. But in the long course of evolution from the seed to the full-grown tree, in the long unfolding of Divinity, of God manifest in the flesh, in the long changing struggle between Spirit and Matter, there the races of mankind stand at different stages of their pilgrimage, and they are not on a common level, but are divorced the one from the other: While in Spirit all men are equal, in the flesh men are radically unequal; for Nature, in her long evolution, knows nothing of equality, and protests continually by facts against the theory of the eighteenth and the early nineteenth century. Where is the equality between the man of genius and the fool? Where is the equality between the stalwart and healthy man and the man who has inherited a terrible disease? Where is the equality between the cripple and the athlete? Between the Saint who has nearly accomplished his pilgrimage, and the savage who stands at the beginning? It is of no use to repeat a phrase that flies in the very face of facts and of Nature. Brotherhood connotes inequality of age, inequality of capacity, and inequality of duty. The duty of the elder brother is not the duty of the babe in the cradle. You do not crush the infant of a year old with the heavy burden of the family that lies on the elder brother, who has passed out into the struggle of life; and you need to get rid of the cant of a phrase and to understand the reality of life. You have to realise that the most that can be asked—because the most that is possible—in the building up of Society, is that no man shall artificially, by a man-made law or custom, be placed at an unfair disadvantage so far as those around him are concerned, but that there shall be equality before the law, equality of rich and poor before the law, equality of every citizen in the face of the law. Moreover, you ought to make it your ideal to give to every man equal opportunities; but you must remember that the radical inequality lies *in the power to grasp an opportunity* when it comes; there is the radical natural inequality that no human society and no human law can obviate.

But if you realise Brotherhood then you come to a new conception. You imagine the building of a social system, in which every man who is born into it shall have the opportunity of developing every faculty he brings with him into the world. A social system wherein from every member of the Society there shall be demanded social service according to his capacity, and to every member shall be given social helping according to his needs. You change the law of struggle into the law of life; you change the brute law of the struggle for existence into the social law of sacrifice. You begin to realise, as Huxley said, quoting a statement of a Master, an Indian Ṛṣhi, that while the brute progresses by the law of the survival of the fittest, the man progresses by the law of self-sacrifice.[1] There

[1] "The law of the survival of the fittest is the law of evolution for the brute; the law of self-sacrifice is the law of evolution for the man."

you come to the higher ideal and you see that in an elder brother there is inequality of age, and therefore inequality of capacity, therefore inequality of power, and therefore inequality of duty. By the law of love, the strong exist not for tyranny but for service, and where the weakest members are found there the tenderest compassion protects them, and saves them from being trampled under foot. Therefore was it said by one of the great Prophets of our race, by the Christ of Judæa: "Let the greatest among you be as he that doth serve." Great is the strength evolved, but for helping not for trampling; and so the inequalities of Nature are redressed by an infinite compassion.

Let us see how in the ancient world these principles, or the denial of these principles, has worked. Now the ancient ideal of Kingship is drawn from the perfect example in the great White Brotherhood of the Ṛṣhis of the race, wherein you find a graded order. They call themselves the "Elder Brothers" of mankind. Those whom we call Masters, because of Their greatness, They love better the name of Elder Brothers on whom lies the duty of guidance, of protection, of helping, in order that the younger brothers of our Humanity may come to stand where They are standing. There is the perfect Brotherhood. These, older in evolution than ourselves, wiser because of that longer evolution, these Jīvanmukṭas, these liberated Spirits, They, who are free by right, become bound to our earth by love. They remain waiting for the growth of Their younger brethren; They use Their wisdom to guide them; They use Their power to protect them; They use Their age to strengthen and sustain them. There is the ideal of Brotherhood, where Brother means the Servant of mankind.

And from that early recognition of the Elders in the childhood of the Root Races of the world, you come to the first great historical exemplification, the Divine Dynasties, the Divine Kings, as you find them in Egypt, as you find them in India, to go no further back to that earlier civilisation of the fourth Race, where in the City of the Golden Gate, of which the Chinese tell us, the Divine Emperor ruled with mighty power, and built the great Toltec race into a world-wide dominion. I will not go back so far, nor will I pause on Egypt, because here, in India, we have in the still living literature of the ancient days, the duties laid down which fall upon the Elder Brother in a Nation, who in those ancient days was the recognised King of the people. You find ideal Kings, like Shrī Rāmachanḍra, and you can see in His life, as you can see in the description of the duty of the King, what, from the standpoint of the Elder Brothers of the race, was meant by the position of the King. His life is not a life of enjoyment, but of service and of sacrifice. It is written, that the King remains awake, in order that his subjects may sleep; that the King toils, in order that his subjects may enjoy; that the King faces danger, in order that his people may be protected; that he is the Supporter of the State, the Guardian of the weak, the Dispenser of Justice to his people, the Father of the fatherless, and the Husband of the widow. And so in early days the Ṛṣhi comes to the court of the King, and questions him how he is ruling his younger brothers. "Have you seen," asked Nāraḍa, when He came to a later dynasty, no longer divine; "have you seen that the artisans are provided with all the materials that they need for their manufactures and industries? Have you seen that the agriculturists have a store of seeds, that they are provided with water, and with agricultural implements? Do you take care that your soldiers receive their wages? Do you take care that the widows and orphans of those who have died for you in battle are well provided for and carefully tended?" And so, this Elder Brother of the race, coming to this man, divine no longer, but only a human copy of the once manifested Divine King, pressed on him the duties of his station, and demanded whether those duties were being rightly exercised. Out of that great ideal of Kingship has grown the reverence for the modern King, though he be of smaller stature, and has not often fulfilled his duties well; for that ideal has printed itself on the heart of mankind, and the passionate love, the intense loyalty, that go out to a King, who is in any sense worthy of Kingship, show how the human heart loves to reverence and to honour, where high power and great position are in any way worthy of the privileges enjoyed.

And always one great warning went out to those ancient Kings, as spoken by Bhīṣhma, the Master of Ḍharma, when the blameless King Yuḍhiṣhthira went to him to ask as to the duties of the Elder Brother of the Nation. He bade him remember that behind the King was the Law, the Divine Law, which none might break with impunity. And then those famous words were spoken that every King should daily remember: "Take care, O King, of the weak, not of the strong; take care of the weak, for the tears of the weak undermine the throne of Kings." That is the great lesson for modern rulers. You may have enemies, you can fight them and conquer them; you may have difficulties, you can surmount them and turn them into steps upwards; but take care of the poor, take care of the miserable, take care of the starving of your realm. For of these, said Bhīṣhma, to whose cry no man listens, the cry enters into the ears of God, who calls on His representative to give account for the miseries of the poor, and who avenges their wrongs by the destruction of the careless King. Now there lies the old ideal.

But many of the States of the past were built on the denial of this great Law of Brotherhood. Look at Babylonia; look at the later Egypt; look at the so-called

Republics of Greece; look at the masses of the people under the Roman Empire; what do you find? You find that every great Empire of the later past has been built on a foundation of the misery of the lowest of the people. You find that the vast majority in these Empires were slaves—slaves in name, as well as in reality. Brotherhood was denied; the weak were trampled on; strength was used to plunder and not to cherish; with the result that every such Empire has faded from the pages of history. When we want to know their stories we have to burrow in their sepulchres, for they built against the Law of Brotherhood, and the Law has broken them into pieces, and they are dead. Now of all the ancient Empires, Babylonia, Assyria, Nineveh, Egypt, Greece, Rome, all these have passed away; only one Nation remains of that splendid circle of civilisations in the past; only one people, contemporary with those mighty Empires, is still a living Nation; they are dead, nay, they are buried, and only the fragments of their bones remain; but one of their contemporaries lives in our modern days, for the India, that traded with Babylonia in the might of her prosperity, is a living Nation in the twentieth century. And why? because in her teaching, because in her religion, because in her literature, she taught the Law of Brotherhood, though later she ceased to live it out in practice, and then began her long downward course. The old theory of the castes was a law of Brotherhood; the Shūḍra who serves, said Manu, he is to be the younger child in your family. There is no humiliation in being a younger child in a family; there is no shame in being one of the juniors of the circle of brothers and sisters; nay, it means the enjoyment of the tenderest compassion; it means a gentle protective attitude; it means that when anything is wanted, the younger shall have what there is and the elder shall go without. That was the old ideal of the Shūḍra, who was to be the young and undeveloped soul. Let him in the National household be the cherished youngling of the family; let him be as your younger son. Then came restrictions with the growing age of the soul. The Vaishya—he was to accumulate wealth; he was to enjoy; he was to be the centre of the great family life, the parent, the supporter of the whole National household. Certainly wealth was to be acquired, but in order to be dispensed—wealth to support the remaining Orders in the State. And that charity that you still find in India, the charity which is of the older days rather than of to-day, is still ingrained in the whole Vaishya caste. For though they will gather wealth—pie by pie, anna by anna, rupee by rupee, they give it away in lakhs and crores for the use of the people. All that is wanted in this charity is to change the direction. There is no use in letting fertilising water run over rocks, because they were once fields; turn it into the fields of to-day, which will then blossom as the rose. I say of the charity of this great wealth-caste, the merchants, the traders, of modern India, that they should turn the wealth they give away so largely into the fertilising streams which will nourish the National fields. Their duty as brothers who are working for the National household, is not only to build temples, to gild the outside of those temples of Ḍevas. What is the use of a temple, if the worshippers are not there? And if you let your youths grope through their studies without knowledge of religion, of what avail to build a temple which will be left empty by them in their manhood? It is the young who need training in religion and in morality, and such education is stopped for lack of the Vaishya liberality. Education is left in the hands of Government, whereas it is the duty of the householders of the Nation. Education under National control, Education in which religion shall form an integral part of the curriculum, that is what India is demanding to-day, and what many are struggling to gain. That Central Hinḍū College which we built in Benares, which has now flowered into the great Hinḍū University, in that you have an attempt, partly frustrated, I admit, to have a University under National control; down in the South, in the great foundation of a merchant of Madras, Pachaiyappa, there you have also the possibility of building up out of a College, a University under National control.

And remember that in this matter, the Indian States under their own Princes are showing the way in which Education should be developed. H. H. the Nizam, the Ruler of Hyderabad, was first of the Indian Princes who gave the order that in every State school in his realm religion should be taught. The religion of Islām to the Musalmāns, the Hindū religion to the Hindūs. And he took our textbooks from the Central Hindū College in order that his Hindū subjects might be taught along liberal orthodox lines; it was a Musalmān Minister of Education who sent out the decree that through the kingdom of Hyderabad every child should be trained in his father's religion, and that religious education should be a part of the duty of the State. And then, H. H. the Maharaja of Mysore took up the same line, and in the State Schools of Mysore religion is an integral part of education. So it is in some of the Rājput States; so it is in some of the Kathiawar States; and these Indian Princes are showing the way to a religious education, that shall be National without being sectarian, that shall not proselytise, that shall not turn boys away from their ancestral faith, but shall respect the religion of the parents, and bring up the children in the faith into which they were born. But you see how the realisation of this needs the charity of the great Vaishya caste, in order that the money may be available which shall make the schools under National control the equals of the Government establishments.

Then, in that caste system, you come to the Kṣhaṭṭriya, from whom more was demanded than from the Vaishya. He had the right to splendour; he had the right to enjoy; he had the right to wealth; but on one condition: he must be willing to sacrifice everything, if the safety of the people demanded it. From him was asked the offering of limb, the offering of life. If he ruled, he must be first in the battle as well as first in the pageant, and he must learn to give up life, family, love, and all that makes life joyous, if the people were in need of protection, and if the order of the State were threatened. And then came the Brāhmaṇa, the teacher, the wise man, the educator of the people. He was not to be wealthy save in wisdom; he was not to gratify desires, but was to be the mouth of God, pure in conduct, ascetic in life; he was to show that the wise man needed not wealth, and that the duty of wisdom was to teach the people. A splendid theory, carried out for many ages. All is in confusion now. The ḍharmas of the castes have broken into pieces, and with the ḍharmas the reality has disappeared. And so the Brāhmaṇa the elder brother, is a lawyer, a merchant, a physician, or anything else, an engine driver sometimes, but seldom a teacher from a sense of ḍharma. And with the old duty, the old reverence has passed away; for only when the elders live up to their duties can the youngers be asked to give them reverence. And so now, Indian Society has to be rebuilt. It has lived, as I have said, because the Law of Brotherhood was its centre, its theory, though its practical denial brought on it the judgment of decay. We find now in our India a mass of conquered people, a slave population in everything but name. The "untouchable" too often goes so foul in body, so foul in speech, in food, that the cleanly shrink from personal contact, and they are left in their foulness, their degradation. But if it be true that the tears of the weak undermine the throne of Kings, what of the denial of Brotherhood which has made this lowest population in our midst? The sweeper, the scavenger, those who perform the hardest duties in Society, they are trampled under foot. India cannot live, if she persist in that denial of Brotherhood, which leaves one section of her population untouchable by the remaining cleanlier people. They were conquered, they were trampled on, they were made outcastes, every foul duty was made their work; they were sacrificed to keep you clean; they were untouchable that you might be refined; they were left in ignorance that you might be educated; and they were degraded that you might be raised. Do you think that the cries of the miserable have not entered into the ears of God? And He looked upon India, and made a stern decree: As you enslave your brethren, you shall yourselves be enslaved.

What ought to be the attitude of Society towards the man, the class, that makes possible cleanliness, refinement and delicacy of life? If you had to clean out your own foul places, if you had to sweep your yards and your streets, would you be as delicate, as refined, as you are to-day? But if these men and women do these humble offices in order that you may live in cleanliness, ought you not to repay them with gratitude and not with contempt, with respect and not with opprobrium? They make your lives possible; your children will have to do these things, your wife and your children, if the scavengers are not there to do the work, and you treat contemptuously those who make possible your civilised life. There lies your crime as a Nation against Brotherhood, and India need not expect to stand high among the Nations of the world, until she sets herself to this work of redeeming her own outcaste population. You are not alone. Other Nations are similar to you. In the country whence my body comes one-tenth of the population is degraded, like your one-sixth. One-tenth of the London population die in the work-house, the prison, the hospital. But I am bound to say to you, though I am sorry to say it, that you remain asleep while England is awake to her duty to her outcaste population, and she is beginning to redeem them from the degradation in which hitherto they have lived. She is educating them, and where education is, there refinement inevitably follows. She is beginning to realise that the lowest work ought to be the shortest. That the lowest work has a right to decent living. That if a man be sacrificed to social necessities, he should be repaid by a leisure which would enable him to live above the degrading tendencies of the necessary surroundings of his work. The British are building houses for them, they are educating their children, they are helping them to live in decency, and so, they are gaining the right to enjoy the freedom they have won. And to you, my Indian brethren, I would say, that if you hold up your hands to Īshvara and pray that liberty may be your own, those hands will never be filled with liberty until you have poured out freedom among your own people, and have begun to redeem your miserable slave population. For Justice is the Divine Law. Those who oppress shall be oppressed; those who trample shall be trampled on; those who make others outcastes shall be outcastes themselves. Until you obey the law of Brotherhood in your dealings with these younger brothers, ignorant, degraded, helpless, you will not win the smile of the Ḍeva of India, nor have His mighty force running upon your side to redeem. But you are waking up, you are beginning to realise your duty. Schools must be scattered over the whole country for the education of the submerged classes; every such school is a temple of Brotherhood, and is quickening the coming of the salvation of the Indian Nation.

And now, finally, what is individual duty as regards Brotherhood? First, to realise that the very condition of the spiritual life is to see the same Self in all equally dwelling. The Self dwells in the outcaste as in the Brāhmaṇa, dwells in the most degraded as in the purest and the noblest; and there is one law of the spiritual life, that as you pour out to others, so shall your own vessel be filled with the water of life. Each of us, then, has a duty as a brother. We are the elders of those younger brothers of our race, and the Law of Brotherhood for the coming Society is, as I said, that every man born into a civilised community shall live under conditions that enable him to develop to the utmost every faculty that he brings with him into the world. That is the law of the coming civilisation. Every child born among you has a right to develop all that he has within him. No obstacles should be placed in his way. Facilities of development should be given. Some are not your equals, but you must not therefore stunt their growth. Every man has the God-given right to develop all that he possesses within him. You must put no artificial barriers. You must make no difficulties which shall be insuperable to them. You must help by virtue of your own longer evolution. You must learn together, in order that you may know the fulness of the Divine Life. But there is this great difference between the life of Matter and the life of Spirit. If on this table

I had a heap of golden coins, and if I said I would give them to you, what a rush there would be for them. But why the rush? Because you know that with every gold mohur given away, there is one less to give away to those who are behind; and so every one wants to be in front, for suppose there is not enough to go round? Sometimes men might try to grasp two or three, so that they may have for the future as well as for the day. It is the law of matter that it perishes in the using; hence there is always struggle; hence it generates divisions, it is the parent of quarrels. But if you knew that there was enough for all, there would be no struggle; if you knew the last would be as the first, there would be no fighting. The law of the Spirit is quite other, for the Spirit lives by giving, not by taking. The Spirit increases by using, he does not waste. As the Spirit has three great aspects of Will, of Consciousness, of Intellect, these are the priceless possessions that we have, and that we can give away without fear of wasting. I have a truth that you have not, and go out and proclaim the truth among you; am I the poorer because you know the truth, or do I know the truth all the better, because in giving it I have appropriated it more thoroughly than I did before? There is no wastage, there is no diminishing; my truth is mine; and when I have given it to every one of you, and you all possess that truth, mine is no lesser. Truth never wastes in the sharing. As you can light one candle from another, and the flame never diminishes though you light a thousand from it, so it is in the case of truth. Knowledge lights new knowledge, so that the total illumination grows greater and not less. Hence if you have knowledge, do not give it among those who already share it, but go out to the ignorant and give it to them. If you are wise, your duty is to make others wise, and not to sit in your own study and enjoy the wisdom as though it were a miser's treasure to gloat over. Knowledge that is not shared becomes a cancer in the brain, and the power to know diminishes and is finally lost, when you refuse to share with your ignorant brother that which you acquired from the boundless stores of Nature. And Purity? Are you pure, in order that you may wrap your garments round you and say to the impure: Stand aside. I will not be polluted. O my friends, the purity that can be polluted is not purity at all, but a garment cast over impurity, hiding it from the world. Purity cannot be soiled; purity cannot be stained; and the duty of the pure is to go out among the impure, in order that they may be purified and lifted to the higher standard. Some I know, would say: "Level down. Pull the educated down. Pull the Brāhmaṇa down. Pull the rich man down. Let us have equality." Equality of what? Of ignorance, of misery, of poverty, of general wretchedness? Nay; lift up the poor to the level of the rich, and let all be comfortable, and none have superfluities. Lift up the ignorant by learning, and so let all be happy in the enjoyment of the treasures of the mind. Go among the sinners, the foul, and the debased, and raise them up to your own purity, and so let the whole nation be pure and educated and healthy and well-fed. And of this be sure—it is written in a Christian Scripture; and is written hundreds of times in your own—"God has made of one blood all the Nations of the earth." Is there one man among you who has not the right to lift up his eyes and say to Brahman: "I am Thou"? Is there one man to whom we can deny the glory of the indwelling Divinity of Spirit? If that be so, and you know it is so, then as your body may have all the life-blood poisoned if a snake sheds his venom into the lowest part of the body; if that poison circles in the blood through all your body, your head and your limbs begin to be paralysed, and your whole body suffers; presently your body will die, though the wound was only in the foot. So it is with the Nation. If the poison is in the foot, in the lowest part of the National body, it spreads through the whole of the Nation, and no part of it is strong. If one man be poor, no rich man is perfectly happy in the enjoyment of his wealth. If one man be ignorant, no wise man can rise to the highest of his mental faculties. If one man be diseased, the health of the whole Nation is lowered. Oh! Nature is always teaching it to you.

Plague begins in a filthy quarter of the town, but it spreads to a palace. In London, in the miserable dwelling of the seamstress, when she makes a ball-dress for a Court Ball, she at times stitches into it her fever, which is the outcome of starvation; and the ball-dress carries it down to the house of a noble, and so it catches the fair daughter of the family. She catches typhoid, and she perishes of the fever generated in the London slum. You cannot separate yourselves; you are brothers whether you will or not. You change your bodies; not one of you will go out of this hall with exactly the same body as you had when you entered it; some particles of your neighbour's body have come into yours. Some of yours have come to me. If you are diseased, you infect others; if you are healthy, your health infects others; if you are drunken, you communicate the poison of drink; if you are plague-stricken, the plague germs run from you to the healthy man. God has so bound us together that we cannot break the chain. Bound as brothers in suffering we must be, if we will not be brothers in love, in health, and in compassion. And so, to you, my brothers, I say: Take heed to yourselves; you stand with the greatest opportunity opening before you, mighty possibilities lie in the near future, which are yours if your hands are pure and your hearts are clean. No Nation has lived, where its poor were despised. The fragments of the past warn you of the dangers of your present. Live the Law of Brotherhood; rescue the miserable; teach the ignorant; feed the starving; nurse the diseased; and, on our India, on her future, the Ḍeva of India shall pour out His blessing, when she lives the law that she has always recognised in theory. That Future shall be mightier than her Past has been, a resurrection of the Spirit, and the spiritualisation of the flesh.

Printed by Annie Besant at the Vasanta Press, Adyar, Madras.